THE LUCKNOW ALBUM

THE LUCKNOW ALBUM

CONTAINING A SERIES OF

FIFTY PHOTOGRAPHIC VIEWS OF LUCKNOW

AND ITS ENVIRONS

TOGETHER WITH A LARGE SIZED

PLAN OF THE CITY

Executed By

DAROGHA UBBAS ALLI

TO THE ABOVE IS ADDED

A FULL DESCRIPTION OF EACH SCENE DEPICTED.

THE WHOLE FORMING A COMPLETE

ILLUSTRATED GUIDE

TO THE CITY OF LUCKNOW

THE CAPITAL OF OUDH

GYAN

Published by

GYAN

Gyan Publishing House
5, Ansari Road
Daryaganj, New Delhi-110002
Phone: 011-47034999, 9811692060
E-mail: books@gyanbooks.com

Distribution Network
gyanbooks.com
India, USA, Canada, UK, Australia, France

ISBN : 978-81-212-9790-5 (HB)
First Published, 1874

2nd Impression 2023

Printed at: Gyan Press, Delhi.

THE LUCKNOW ALBUM
Author: DAROGHA UBBAS ALLI

THE

LUCKNOW ALBUM.

CONTAINING A SERIES OF

FIFTY PHOTOGRAPHIC VIEWS OF LUCKNOW

AND ITS ENVIRONS

TOGETHER WITH A LARGE SIZED

PLAN OF THE CITY

EXECUTED BY

DAROGHA UBBAS ALLI,

Assistant Municipal Engineer.

TO THE ABOVE IS ADDED

A FULL DESCRIPTION OF EACH SCENE DEPICTED.

THE WHOLE FORMING A COMPLETE

ILLUSTRATED GUIDE

TO THE CITY OF LUCKNOW

THE CAPITAL OF OUDH.

1874.

Dedicated by Permission

TO

SIR GEORGE COUPER, BART., C. B.,

CHIEF COMMISSIONER OF OUDH.

CONTENTS.

INTRODUCTION.

Ruins, ancient and modern, bearing marks of oriental splendour and extravagance; the relics of Monarchies now passed away: prostrate columns, broken arches, colonnades, fountains, statues, shattered and shot-battered walls, scathed monuments, telling of the horrors of war, rebellion and siege; neglected gardens and roofless, dismantled palaces, fast falling into decay, are all objects of interest and curiosity to the tourist, the antiquary, the historian, the archæologist and the lover of art. The city of Lucknow, the capital of Oudh, abounds with objects of this description in all the intense sublimity of ruin, and evincing the stern decrees of fate that have thus destined them to destruction, and that, but for the present volume, would have ruthlessly consigned them to everlasting oblivion. The thrilling historical or traditionary narratives that from time to time have been published, and the glowing descriptions that have been given by travellers, have, since railway communication became available, had the effect of considerably increasing the number of visitors; the want of an "Illustrated Album," that should also act as a guide, being consequently felt, the present volume has been prepared, at great expense, and profusely illustrated, to supply that want, and the projectors hope that it will succeed in fostering the spirit of enquiry, to which the histories of the objects afore mentioned have so manifestly given birth, and to which the educated Natives of India and the travelling public of all nations throughout the civilized world are so much attached.

It has already been remarked that, to the general traveller or tourist, the work will prove of great interest; it may be added that, to some, it will be of inestimable value; but to the friends and relations of the survivors, and to the survivors themselves, of the terrible rebellion of 1857-58, especially to those who were actual members of the beleaguered Garrison at the Lucknow Residency; whose gallant and glorious defence against overwhelming forces of a cruel, fanatical and barbarous foe, preserved the prestige of the British arms at such fearful sacrifices, this work will not prove an intellectual treat alone; the scenes herein depicted will revive old memories falling sadly but proudly on the heart; memories of the mighty dead, of brave sons and fathers, of dear sisters, loving wives and sweet children, who now sleep peacefully in the midst of the ruined grandeur where they fell. To the survivors of that Garrison, this Album will bear a sacred interest, and many a tear will fall at the contemplation of some well-remembered spot, over which a sort of holy radiance will appear to linger as the book is sorrowfully closed. The volume may be preserved, for transmission to posterity, as a memorial of the dangers passed and the hardships suffered by the glorious Garrison of Lucknow.

The Album being intended to serve as a pictorial guide, cannot be expected to contain profuse historical accounts of the scenes represented dating back from ages of remote antiquity: trusting rather to the silent eloquence of modern illustration aided by photography, which, with talismanic power, appeals to the senses of old and young of all nations and tongues, or in the words of the poet:—

> "Sounds, which address the ear, are lost, and die
> In one short hour; but those which strike the eye
> Live long upon the mind; the faithful sight
> Engraves the knowledge with a beam of light."

The projectors respectfully beg that, in consideration of the work having been produced, regardless of pains or expense, and under great difficulties, as regards shortcomings, the public will be lenient and the critics merciful; and trusting that it may meet with approval, the "Lucknow Album" is sent forth to meet its fate.

LUCKNOW ALBUM.

THE CITY.

THE city of Lucknow was, for a long time, renowned for its riches and flourishing trade. The city proper is said to occupy the site of the debris of some threescore villages, the names of many of which are perpetuated in the several *Mohullas* which are called after them, but of themselves not the slightest trace remains. It is built on irregular, undulating ground, intersected by watercourses, *nullahs* and ravines. Its antiquity is questionable, but only about ninety years have elapsed since, from its ancient rival, Fyzabad, it usurped the title and dignity of "Capital of Oudh," and it is not a little remarkable that, in so comparatively short a period, it should have assumed such proportions as to extend, with its suburbs, over an area of twenty square miles.

There is a tradition that Fyzabad or Ajoodia, and Lucknow, the distance between the two being some seventy odd miles, were once united by a series of small towns, formming one continuous and gigantic city; another tradition asserts that the two cities were formerly connected by a secret subterranean passage, known only to the Kings of Oudh. These traditions are only worth mentioning, as showing the singular credulity for which the natives of Oudh are remarkable. The stories are of course thoroughly fabulous.

Prior to the annexation of the kingdom of Oudh, Lucknow consisted mostly of strong masonry built houses in the usual fantastic mixture of Italian and Mahomedan architecture, two or three stories high, forming narrow, but picturesque, streets: the bazars were abundantly stocked, the population was literally "teeming," so that it was impossible to ride, or drive, in the streets, save at a walk; the people generally were cleanly dressed, betokening that they were living under a regime, which placed the common necessaries of life reasonably within the reach of all classes; but the melancholy and memorable events of 1857-58 have reduced the number of handsome houses by one half, whilst the trade and manufactures, for which, in all their riches and variety, Lucknow was once so famous, have all but disappeared. Nevertheless, to compensate for this apparent deterioration, there are now many fine broad streets, many excellent market-places, improved ventilation, good drainage; and seemingly a more equable and healthy air of prosperity may well be hoped for, especially when the traffic becomes developed by the completion of the Oudh and Rohilkund network of railways, The traveller may then bid farewell to the crumbling mosque, the deserted garden, the ruined fountain, the remains of palaces, seraglios and all the marks of the reigns of the kings of Oudh. Lucknow will gradually assume its former prosperity as the veritable capital.

THE PRINCIPAL BUILDINGS, GARDENS, &c.

Approaching the city by rail from Cawnpore, commencing from a southerly direction, the first view is that of—

AULUM BAGH,

Nos. 1 and 2.

This was originally a fortified garden, containing a large summer-house and out-offices, built and arranged, as an occasional residence, for Newab Khas Mehal, wife of the ex-king, Wajid Ali Shah, Sultana Aulum.

During the late rebellion, the garden was occupied by a strong force of rebel troops, who held the place up to the 23rd September, 1857, when, after a desperate defence, it was captured by General Havelock, and converted into a depôt for the sick and wounded, numbering some 400, of the British force. The General then, accompanied by the chivalrous Outram, undertook his gallant advance to reinforce, or finally rescue, the long beleaguered garrison of the Bailie Guard.

The Aulum Bagh derives a melancholy interest from the circumstance of the remains of the late lamented General Havelock having been buried there. The monument, "view No. 2," erected to his memory, stands, overshadowed by trees, in a quiet corner, and is extremely modest in size and pretensions.

The honor and gallantry of the General were so far rewarded, that he lived to see the object for which he had fought so bravely, successfully accomplished: it was not until the sick and wounded, and the women and children, had been safely escorted from the besieged Bailie Guard, to the camp of the Commander-in-Chief at Mahomed Bagh, that the noble spirit of the Christian soldier succumbed to disease, brought on by incessant exposure and anxiety. The monument bears the following inscription :—

"HERE REST THE MORTAL REMAINS OF

HENRY HAVELOCK,

"Major-General in the British Army and Knight Commander of the Bath; who died, at Dilkoosha, Lucknow, of dysentery, produced by the hardships of a campaign, in which he achieved immortal fame, on the 24th November, 1857. He was born on the 5th April, 1795, at Salops, Monmouth, county Durham, England."

"Entered the Army in 1815, came to India in 1823, and served there, with little interruption, until his death. He bore an honorable post in the wars of Burma, Affghanistan, the Maharatta Campaign of 1843, and the Sutlej of 1845-46. Retained, by adverse circumstances, during many years, in a subordinate position, it was the aim of his life to prove, that the profession of a Christian is consistent with the fullest discharge of the duties of a soldier."

He commanded a division in the Persian expedition of 1857. In the terrible convulsion of that year, his genius and character were, at length, fully developed and known to the world. Saved from shipwreck on the Ceylon Coast, by that Providence which designed him for yet greater things, he was nominated to the command of the column destined to relieve the brave garrison of Lucknow. This object of almost superhuman exertions he, by the blessing of God, accomplished, but he was not spared to receive on earth the reward so dearly earned; and the Divine Master whom he served, saw fit to remove him from the sphere of his labours, in the moment of his greatest triumph.

He departed to his rest in humble, but confident expectation of far greater rewards and honors than those which a grateful country was anxious to bestow on him. The skill of a commander, the courage and devotion of a soldier, the learning of a scholar, the grace of a high-bred gentleman, and all the social and domestic virtues of a husband, father, and friend, were blended together, strengthened, harmonized and adorned by the spirit of a true Christian—the result of the influence of the Holy Spirit on his heart and of a humble reliance on the merits of a crucified Saviour.

"I have fought a good fight, I have finished my course,
"I have kept the faith: henceforth there is laid up for me
"a crown of righteousness, which the Lord, the Righteous
"Judge, shall give me on that day; and not to me only,
"but to all those that love His appearing."

" His ashes in a peaceful urn shall rest;
His name a great example stands, to show
How strangely high endeavours may be blessed,
When piety and valour jointly go."

This monument is erected by his sons, widow and family.

BEBEAPORE KI KOTHE.

VIEW No. 3.

At a spot, a few miles eastward of the city, stand the ruins of the old palace of Bebeapore. Newab Ausuf-ood-dowlah, the first of the Newabs who made Lucknow the capital, built this palace as a country residence, and enclosed a park, in which an immensity of small game was preserved. Whenever a change of residents, or political agents, to the King's Court, took place, the new arrival always had this palace placed at his disposal, until he should be conducted in state to the Residency in the city. It was from here that went forth the memorable decree of the Government of India for the deposition of Wuzeer Ali, the adopted son and heir of Ausuf-ood-dowlah. Wuzeer Ali was subsequently removed to Benares, where he became notorious as the murderer of Mr. Cherry, the Governor-General's Agent. It was here also that Lord Teignmouth held a grand Durbar, the object of which was, to obtain the enthronement of Newab Saadut Ali Khan, in succession te Wuzeer Ali. The object was attained, and the reign of Saadut Ali Khan proved eminently successful.

The palace might still be so far repaired as to be inhabitable, but there does not, at present, appear to be any special way in which it could be utilized. The park is utterly neglected, and is now infested with wild animals.

On the road from Bebeapore to the city is—

THE WELAITE BAGH.

VIEW NO. 4.

The summer house in this garden was erected by King Naseer-ood-deen Hyder, and the grounds were laid out by him and planted with European plants, principally; hence its designation. It lies on the banks of the river Goomtee and was, in the King's time, a very handsome pleasure-garden. It was a favourite resort of the King, who used to proceed thero by water, accompanied by the members of his Court, in pleasure-boats, by night. The garden is not remarkable on account of any historical associations; it is the station regatta winning-post; it has fallen into neglect, but still retains some remnants of its original beauty.

We next come to the—

DILKOOSHA.

VIEW NO. 5.

This magnificent hunting-box, or country-seat, was built by Saadut Ali Khan. He cleared away the dense jungle surrounding it, and converted the grounds into an immense, well-arranged park, which he stocked with deer and other game, and further so beautifully ornamented the place, that it became the favourite resort of the ladies of the court during the summer months.

During the siege of the Bailie Guard, in 1857, the Dilkoosha was held, in great force, by the enemy, but on the 14th November it was captured by Sir Colin Campbell, when he advanced to the relief of the beleaguered Garrison.

After the formation of the new Cantonment, at Mahomed Bagh, the Dilkoosha was made a residence for the General commanding the Division, and remained so for years; but it has lately been dismantled, and although it is built on an eminence, nothing can now be seen of the once noble edifice, but its bare massive walls and castellated stair-cases. It was on the western slope of the approach to this building, that the rescued Garrison of the Bailie Guard bivouacked, on the night of the 30th November, and attempted to rest their weary limbs, while prevented from sleeping by the tremendous cannonading kept up by the enemy.

Not far from this spot, to the northward, is that grand and noble pile of buildings known as—

LA MARTINIERE.

View No. 6.

Called "*La Martiniere*" after the name of its illustrious founder, General Claude Martin of the King of Oudh's service. It is also called "Constantia." Its construction was commenced during the reign of Newab Ausuf-ood-dowlah who, when it was nearly completed, became so pleased with the design of the structure, that he offered to purchase it as it stood for a million sterling. It is not certain whether the General accepted the offer; however, the bargain was broken off by the death of the Newab, and the General also died, before the building was finished, not, however, before he had made a provision in his will, to the effect that it should be completed out of the funds that he had left in the hands of the British Government, for the special endowment of schools. The building was accordingly finished, and the magnificent pile, with its establishment, now known as "La Martiniere College," stands as an elegant and lasting monument to the memory of one of the greatest benefactors of the youth, of all creeds and colours, that call India their home. The remains of the General were buried in a vault in the centre of the building. During the rebellion of 1857-58, the mutineers dug up this vault, in the hope of finding treasure; they were disappointed, and, it seems, in the height of their rage, scattered the bones of the General about in derisive contempt. When the position was recaptured, part of the remains were found, and reverently restored to their resting-place. A towering pillar of solid masonry, standing in the middle of an artificial lake adjoining the massive pile, also perpetuates the memory of the great man.

General Claude Martin was a native of Lyons: he came to India, as a soldier, under Lally, in 1760, and after the surrender of Pondicherry, was appointed to the charge of a Company of French pioneers, who had been formed into a Company of Chasseurs. About 1780, he came to Lucknow, and Newab Seraj-ood-dowlah offered him the command of the Artillery; he accepted the offer, with the consent of the Hon. East India Company, and acquired the rank of Major General. He died in 1800, after accumulating several millions sterling, the bulk of which he bequeathed to the most noble and charitable purposes.

The canal, which has now to be crossed, is only so far worthy of mention; that it was commenced during the reign of King Nuseer-ood-deen Hyder. It was intended to run from the Ganges for the purpose of irrigating the country between Lucknow and Cawnpore; but barely a few miles had been excavated when funds failed, the greater portion of the sums expended having been misappropriated by the contractors, who fled, with their dishonestly acquired fortunes, away from the kingdom.

This stupendous ditch, however, afforded the rebels in 1857, a strong line of defence on the southern and eastern sides of the city, and Sir Colin Campbell's force, when advancing to the relief of the Residency, had hot work in crossing the awkward gap.

Having crossed the canal, the entrance to the city is from the eastern quarter ; and immediately to the left will be found—

HYAT BUKSH.

View No. 7.

The residence of the Chief Commissioner. This house was built by Nawab Saadut Ali Khan, and was, during the reign of Nuseer-ood-deen Hyder, occupied by Colonel Roberts of the Oudh Service. Upon annexation, Major Banks, Commissioner of Lucknow, became the occupant, hence it was, during the mutiny, known as "Banks' house;" it occupies a very conspicuous position, and the rebels had a strong hold of it, until the 18th March, 1858, when it was taken by a detachment of troops under command of Sir Edward Lugard. Lately the building has been much enlarged and improved, and the garden elegantly laid out. This work was commenced in 1873, at which time Sir George Couper, Bart. C. B., C. S., was Officiating Chief Commissioner of Oudh.

There is a certain melancholy interest attaching to the house, on account of the gallant Hudson having breathed his last within its walls. He had just despatched, on his own responsibility, at a most critical moment, certain of the Delhi Princes who, it was well known, were dangerous foes to the British.

Across the road, on the right, is an imposing building that could hardly be believed to be devoted to the purposes of trade : it is occupied by Messrs. Peake, Allen and Company, an enterprising firm of merchants.

A little onward is the—

DARUL SHAFFA.

View No. 8.

This house, as its name implies, is a Hospital or Dispensary, which was built by Newab Saadut Ali Khan, and was intended for the reception of the indigent sick, but was never used for that purpose. It is said that some of the ladies of the Oudh Court, having conceived a fancy, obtained possession, and made use of it as a place affording retirement, where they could hold occasional merry-makings in secret. The house has been thoroughly renovated, and is now the residence of the Secretary to the Chief Commissioner, and may be considered one of the most enviable residences in Lucknow.

Immediately on the right commences a long range of buildings, the whole together known as the Begum Kothi. In the days of the King, these comprised the palace of the Queen mother of Oudh. After the departure of Her Majesty to Europe, in 1856, the buildings remained occupied, strictly as a zenana enclosure, by members of the Queen's household; but, during the mutiny, the rebels took possession and garrisoned them. On the reoccupation of Lucknow by the British, they each had to be taken by storm. The high wall was levelled, and the several fine buildings, which were hidden from view, have been converted into handsome shops and public offices. The first is, the shop of Messrs. Nowrjee and Company; the next is the extensive printing establishment of Moonshee Newul Kishore; a press that, from the large quantity of work carried on, is, in all probability, the largest in India. Next is the shop of Messrs. Cursetjee's sons, and adjoining is the Government Post Office, formerly an *Imambarra*, or mausoleum; it is reported that in this building the late Post Master, Mr. Mackenzie, discovered a quantity of hidden treasure. The next conspicuous object is Mr. Joseph Paton's celebrated clock-tower: it contains no clock, because a portion of the machinery was stolen, and as the building has since passed into other hands, the empty tower remains to mark the memory of the builder.

The most imposing structure in Huzrutgunge is—

THE OFFICES OF THE OUDH AND ROHILKUND RAILWAY COMPANY.

VIEW No. 9.

A short time after the recapture of Lucknow, a detachment of Royal Horse Artillery, located in this building, discovered treasure, to the amount of some three or four lacs of rupees, while driving pegs in the ground to picket their horses but what became of the treasure, is still a mystery. The agent of the Railway Company now holds office here.

The next building, or range, is occupied by Messrs. Murray and Company, merchants, and Madame Lines' millinery establishment.

On the opposite side of the street is the Roman Catholic Chapel, or—

ST. JOSEPH'S CHURCH.

VIEW No. 10.

This beautiful chapel was brought into existence by subscription from the Roman Catholic community of the Civil Lines; its neat appearance and cleanliness speak well for the energy of the Chaplain, Father Lewis. Further on towards Huzrutgunge, are the coach manufactory of Messrs. Hormusjee and Company, Messrs. Conway and Company, and Messrs. Sinclair and Company; going on to the eastward, past the well-stocked bazar of Huzrutgunge, through the handsome shady trees will be seen the graceful spire of—

CHRIST'S CHURCH.

VIEW No. 11.

Built by the Protestant cammunity under the superintendence of Lieutenant Swetenham, R. E. The church is built in the modern style of architecture. The Reverend Mr. Moore is the present popular and much respected incumbent.

Further on, a little to the eastward, is the—

WINGFIELD PARK.

VIEW No. 12.

This Park, originally called Banarsee Bagh, was in a very dilapidated state, when it came into possession of the British. It is now named after the late popular Chief Commissioner of Oudh, who took advantage of the natural picturesqueness of the spot, to have it carefully beautified with beds of flowers, umbrageous trees, *parterres*, gravelled walks and drives, &c., &c. This park, though not very extensive, is equal in beauty to any in this part of India. It affords shade and accommodation for fancy fairs, flower and vegetable shows, and archery meetings.

The marble *baradurree* was once the pride of Huzrut Bagh. It was removed and rebuilt where it now stands, a graceful and elegant work of art, in the centre of the flower garden. This magnificent building is said, like the Taj at Agra, to have been inlaid with precious stones; it appears they have all been removed, for nothing but counterfeit imitations now supply their place.

Returning through Huzrutgunge and turning to the right, the building vulgarly known as the "*Chowper Stables,*" is seen at a short distance. In this building, the choicest of the King's horses and equipages used to be kept; it was considered decidedly stylish for such a purpose. After the annexation it became the barracks of H. M.'s 32nd Light Infantry. During the mutiny, the rebels converted the range into an arsenal, where they attempted to make percussion caps and other kind of ammunition; it is believed they were not very successful.

It was a work of great difficulty to capture these buildings after the reoccupation; the enemy fought desperately, and Sir Colin Campbell's force suffered severely in the engagement.

After the mutiny, the buildings were partitioned off into quarters for uncovenanted clerks and others; the grounds have been turned into gardens, and the building is now ostentatiously termed "Lawrence Terrace;" a more appropriate name would be the "Writers' Buildings" of Lucknow.

The straight road leads to the—

SEKUNDER BAGH.

VIEW No. 13.

This garden may be very well described as the "*Shalimar*" of Lucknow. It was built by Wajid Ali Shah, especially in honor of one of his favourite *mehals*, Sekunder Begum; hence its name. It is encircled by a high wall, and has earned an imperishable page in history as the death-place of more than two thousand mutineers who were bayonetted without mercy, by the exasperated British troops under command of Sir Colin Campbell, on the 16th of November, 1857. The rebels, within the high loop-holed wall, had every advantage in repulsing our troops; the assault of the British was gallant in the extreme, and many a brave British soldier fell, before the stronghold was captured.

Wheeling to the left along the road, the Company Bagh is seen on the right; this is a nursery for a great variety of fruit trees and vegetables.

A short distance further on, is the—

KUDDUM RASOOL.

VIEW NO. 14.

This is a shrine sacred to the Mahomedans, it was built by King Ghazee-ood-deen Hyder: it stands on the summit of a mound, and is believed to contain a stone, bearing the foot-print of the Prophet Mahomed. The stone is said to have been brought from Mecca by some distinguished pilgrim.

During the mutiny, the place afforded a strong position for the rebels, but was soon taken by the British. It is not a little singular that the building should be held in such reverence by the Mahomedans; for a report is extant, to the effect that the sacred stone has been stolen; the shrine therefore contains nothing to venerate.

A little further on, is—

NAJUF ASHRUF OR SHAH NAJAF,

VIEW NO. 15.

Or the mausoleum of King Ghazee-ood-deen Hyder, built by himself, for the interment of his own remains. It is surrounded by a high wall, and, like the Kuddum Rasool, afforded the mutineers an excellent position for defence. It was here that poor Sir William Peel, Commander of the Naval Brigade, earned an imperishable renown. This brave sailor, covered by the fire of two heavy guns, and supported by a small body of Infantry, literally scaled the high wall and jumped down into the midst of the enemy in the enclosure; his men followed his example, and in spite of the immense superiority of the force they fell amongst, succeeded in dealing terrific slaughter, the ship's cutlass being the only weapon used. The place was soon after occupied by the British troops under command of Brigadier General Sir Adrian Hope.

The place derives the name "Najuf," from the hill on which the tomb of Ali, the son-in-law of Mahomed, is built, of which tomb this is said to be an exact copy.

A fund was left by King Ghazee-ood deen Hyder, to keep the place in repair, to illuminate it yearly on the anniversary of his death, and to maintain an establishment. It is a place of great sanctity with the Mahomedans, but is not so grand as the great Imambara of Hosainabad which will be noticed in due course.

At a short distance, on the same road, is the—

MOTE MAHAL.

VIEW No. 16.

This building was constructed by Newab Saadut Ali Khan: it owes its name to a superstructural projection, not a dome, in a semi-almond form, without any timber supports, but entirely of masonry, which gave the fancied resemblance to the curve of a pearl: this answers to the word "Mote."—Mahal can only be translated as "seraglio," or, "*Zenana Khana*;" the whole name, then, amounts to, the "Pearl Seraglio." It never was used as a seraglio, and appears to have been built for purposes of defence, or check, on the advance of an enemy; in short, it may be described as the *beau-ideal* of a miniature citadel: it is prettily situated on the banks of the Goomtee, and is connected with a range of buildings known as the "Mubarik Munzil" and the "Shah Munzil." These buildings were appropriated to no particular purposes; except the last-named, from which the King used to witness wild sports, of the Spanish Bull fight, or the Roman Coliseum, order. The smaller wild beasts used to fight within the enclosure; here also tiger combats were indulged in; but the elephant and rhinoceros encounters, which had to be viewed at a safe distance, were performed on the opposite side of the Goomtee, on level ground in front of Hazaree Bagh. The British Resident, no doubt much to his disgust, used out of courtesy to attend these exhibitions.

Upon the annexation of the province, the "Mote Mahal" was used temporarily as a Commissariat store. It has since been purchased from Government by the Maharajah of Bulrampore, who has entirely changed the aspect of the buildings and of the surrounding country; the "pearl dome," formed in defiance of all mathematical rules of architecture, has disappeared, and the buildings comprising the "Mote Mahal" have assumed a grand Baronial appearance, in keeping with their romantic history.

Like all other buildings on record, the "Mote Mahal" was enclosed by a high wall and, in 1857, was strongly fortified by the rebels. It had, like the rest, to be taken by storm, which was accomplished by Sir Colin Campbell, who made it a depôt for heavy guns and spare stores. It was here that Brigadier General Cooper commanding the Artillery, Lieutenant Crumb, Madras Artillery, and Dr. Bartram lost their lives; Colonel Campbell also received a wound that, in a few days, proved mortal. One, however, was fortunate, that was Private Duffy, of H. M.'s 90th, who recaptured a gun that the enemy had taken, for which act of gallantry he was rewarded with the V. C.

On the left of the road will be seen the—

KHOORSHAID MUNZIL.

View No. 17.

This building, as will be seen from the view, is castellated and surrounded by a deep scarped ditch; intended evidently for purposes of defence. The structure was commenced by Saadut Ali Khan, and finished by Ghazee-ood-deen Hyder: the purpose that these monarchs had, when designing such a palpable stronghold, is difficult to surmise, and a study of their histories fails to show the necessity of such a building; especially, since the Kings of Oudh declared that they considered their country perfectly secure under the guaranteed protection of the British Government. The Kings of Oudh never made any use of the building, but when the mutiny broke out, it was strongly fortified, and occupied in force by the rebels. It took a great many hours' cannonading, before it was taken by the storming party, consisting of the Naval Brigade and detachments from the 90th and 53rd Regiments, when it was stoutly defended by the mutineers.

The Khoorshaid Munzil is entitled to a name in history, as being the meeting place of the succouring and the relieving Generals, Outram and Havelock of the former, and Sir Colin Campbell of the latter: it was here that they shook hands and congratulated each other on the extraordinary success of their arms over the overwhelming forces and apparently impregnable defences of the enemy.

As a contrast to the purpose that the Khoorshaid Munzil was probably intended to serve, and the demoniac purpose that it did attempt to serve, it is now turned to a heavenly purpose: it is the Martiniere Girls' School; the scarped ditch is now a bright green lawn for the children's play-ground, the towers make airy bedrooms for the little girls, and all the inmates seem to be supremely happy.

Adjoining is the—

TARA KOTHE OR STAR HOUSE.

VIEW NO. 18.

The reason why this was called the Star House is, that it was intended for an observatory. It forms a kind of set-off to the general extravagance for which the Kings of Oudh were notorious. Nusseer-ood-deen Hyder had this house constructed under European superintendence, and provided with astronomical instruments of value, but, from the observations taken, nothing in the service of science seems to have resulted: the instruments were all demolished by the mutineers, and the King always thought more of astrology than of astronomy. So much for the enlightenment of the Monarchs of Oudh.

There was a native of Fyzabad known as Moulvie Ahmodollah Shah, who always had a drum beaten before him wherever he went, and was consequently called "Dunka Shah;" he made the Khoorshaid Munzil his Head Quarters, and the Moulvie being of high reputation amongst the Mahomedans, the house soon became a sort of Baradurree for parliamentary meetings: however, after the mutiny, finding the country too hot to hold him, he disappeared, and the house became a rebel stronghold; this was stormed and captured by Sir Colin Campbell's force in 1857, the high wall that surrounded it, was demolished, and there now appears, on its mound, the handsome building known as the Bank of Bengal.

On the southern side is an extensive space called the "Place Road," and close by, on the right, stands a very modest unpretending looking obelisk. This is the—

MEMORIAL OF THE MASSACRE OF EUROPEAN CAPTIVES.

VIEW No. 19.

Which commemorates the most calamitous and, perhaps, the most cruel incident in the whole history of the rebellion of 1857-58. It was on this spot that Miss Jackson, Sir Mountstuart Jackson, Mrs. Green, Mrs. Rogers, Captain Patrick Orr, Lieutenant Burns, Mr. Carew, Mr. J. Sullivan and Sergeant Morton, with other persons, captured in the town, and some deserters from the Bailie Guard, were deliberately slaughtered in cold blood. The miscreant, Rajah Jey-lal Singh, who witnessed and instigated this cruel massacre, was, some years afterwards, convicted of the crime, on the evidence of his own followers, and was executed in sight of the spot where stands the memorial of the foul deed: his wife offered five lacs of rupees for a commutation of the sentence, but the offer was indignantly refused; his estates and property were confiscated, and in this world no greater punishment could be inflicted upon him.

Towards the left is the Ainuk Baz ke-kothee, next is a pretty building, the Delhi and London Bank. Adjoining is the—

KUNKUR WALI KOTHI.

VIEW NO. 20.

During the mutiny, this building was made the Head Quarters of the rebel General, Burkat Ahmud; as to who built it, or what use it was formerly put to, history is conflicting: at present it is occupied by Captain Pitcher, Judge of the Small Cause Court.

On the right is a large building, formerly used as a church: it is the tomb of Amjud Ali Shah, the fourth King of Oudh, and is commonly called "*Junnut Makan ka Imambarra.*"

Turning again towards the Obelisk, on arriving at the end of the street, is seen the—

NOOR BUKSH-KI-KOTHI,

OR

LIGHT GIVING HOUSE.

VIEW NO. 21.

So named because, when illuminated, from its great height it lighted up the neighbourhood for miles around:

it was built by Newab Saadut Ali Khan and became the residence of one of his sons. Sir Henry Havelock took advantage of this building, and, from it, saw his way through the enemy's third line of defences so as to effect an entrance into Kaiser Bagh: the enemy detected him in the act, and until lately, the walls of that house bore the marks of a shower of grape aimed at him from the guns below.

Immediately at the back is Zahoor Buksh-ke-Kothee, another Imambarra, now the premises of the Church Mission Press. These buildings, together with the one on the opposite side of the road, formed one enclosure surrounded by high walls. During the rebellion the place was occupied by the enemy in great force, and had to be taken by storm. The walls have since been demolished; and the whole place being opened out, and the different edifices almost entirely rebuilt, no trace of its original appearance remains.

Entering now the Kaiser Baugh by the Northern gate, or archway, through which the unfortunate captives, Sir Mountstuart Jackson, and the rest, were led to a savage and barbarous massacre, an open court has to be passed, called "*Jelloo Khana*," or place where Royal Processions used to parade and form up in preparation to start: then to the right, through another archway, the Chenee Baugh appears; so called from the circumstance of its having been ornamented with China, or what appeared to be China, vessels; another archway, flanked by green mermaids, leads into "Huzrut Baugh." On the right is the "Chandeewalee Barradurree" so named from the fact of the columns and roof having been, originally, covered with silver, the whole of which was torn off and appropriated by the rebels of 1857 notoriety, anxious to plunder alike friend and foe: afterwards, the Chandeewalee Barradurree became the office of the *Oudh Gazette*, now extinct, and the building has been sold to a private individual.

There was a building on this spot, called Khas Makan, used by the ladies of the Court, but, as it has been pulled down, and the ground, upon which it stood, levelled, it is needless to relate its history, it must sink into oblivion, according to the fate of works produced by human ; hands this work only professes to treat of the histories of such as remain, either intact, or in ruins.

Close by, "*Badshah Munzil*" is seen. This building was used by the King as the Council-house, for the State reception of the British Resident, it was in those days finely decorated; but it was here that General Outram read the stern decree of Government, by which the kingdom of Oudh was inexorably annexed, and the monarchy was put an end to. Because the ex-king ceased to be King from this house, the natives call it the "*Gharut Munzil*," or, "*desolated house*."

The quarters over the mermaid archway, just passed, were originally occupied by Nawab Ali Naki Khan, *primi mortis*, so that he might be close to the King, and thereby have the earliest opportunity of knowing all that was going on. The buildings adjoining were the residences of the chief mehals; and afterwards the Rebel Begum, Huzrut Mehal, held her court there. In the stables near that place, the British captives were kept for some weeks.

Further on, the great "Lackhee Gate or archway," so called from its having cost a lakh of rupees in building, is passed, and then a magnificent quadrangle opens to the view ; this is the celebrated—

KAISER BAGH, OR CÆSAR'S GARDEN.

VIEWS NOS. 22 TO 24.

Or the famous palace of the ex-King, Wajid Ali Shah Sultan-a-Aulum. This great palace was commenced by the ex-King in the year 1850, and, in his wild ambition to have a palace of surpassing grandeur, he had it completed in the shortest time possible, at a cost of more than a million sterling. The principal part of the palace comprised the great rectangle, the buildings surrounding which would provide quarters for upwards of a thousand *Mehals*, or Queens; there were many other detached buildings also forming part of the palace; each building was provided with a private garden of its own, the whole was enclosed by a high masonry wall, and the gardens, in the centre of the square, were most tastfully laid out and adorned with innumerable fountains; the walks were lined with classic statuary, the surrounding buildings were sumptuously furnished and richly decoratad with large chandeliers, girandoles, wall brackets, furniture elaborately mounted in silver and gold, embroidered curtains, Cashmere tapestry: everything calculated to add to the splendour of an Oriental Court was brought into requisition, no matter what the cost, or from what distance the articles had to be brought. This, like the flickering of a lamp, was the last attempt of the monarchs of Oudh, to make themselves great amongst nations; it was a brilliant attempt, but not sufficiently dazzling to deceive the British Government.

Although long since deserted by royalty, the remains of the palace are still magnificent ruins in a good state of preservation, but from a present view, no adequate idea of what the original *tout ensemble* resembled, can be conveyed. The buildings composing the main rectangle have been made over to the *Talookdars*, or Barons, of Oudh, who make use of some portions as dwelling-houses, leaving the remainder as roofless and dismantled walls, presenting to the view a striking reminiscence of oriental grandeur and extravagance converted into a desolate waste. The great arched entrances still remain with their massive gates in bronze, bearing on their panels, in *basso relievo*, representations of the mermaid and the royal insignia of the King of Oudh.

In fighting their way towards the Bailie Guard, the Kaiser Bagh was one of the strongest positions our troops had to take: the buildings were crowded with mutineers who had loaded themselves with plunder, the spoil of the richest seraglio in the world: the British troops rushed into the rooms and, with bayonet and bullet, slaughtered without mercy the luckless rebels, making them disgorge their ill-gotten plunder which was scattered about in reckless confusion, mingled with their blood.

Between the great quadrangle of Kaiser Bagh, and China Bazar, stand two mausoleums of imposing size and grandeur, these are—

SAADUT ALI KHAN'S TOMB, AND MOORSHED ZADI'S TOMB.

VIEWS NOS. 25 AND 26.

The *Mukara*, or tomb, of Nawab Saádut Ali Khan, has since his death been called, by apotheosis, "*Junnut Aramgah*," or the house of one whose soul reposes in paradise. The other tomb is that of Moorshed Zadi, the Queen of Saadut Ali Khan.

The spot on which these tombs now stand, was formerly occupied by a house in which Ghazee-ood-deen Hyder, son of Saadut Ali Khan, resided. History says that, when the son came to the throne in the father's place, he remarked that, since he had taken his father's house, it was but fair that he should give up his own to his father and mother; accordingly he gave orders for his former abode to be destroyed, and for the two mausoleums, under description, to be built on the site. The Royal Family of Oudh never displayed any remarkable traits of filial affection, so that, admitting the truth of this tradition, Ghazee-ood-deen Hyder must have been an exception to the general rule. The resting-place of some ten or fifteen British soldiers, who lost their lives by an explosion, is marked on a spot between the two tombs.

Close by is the square called Huzrut Bagh. This contained a *tykhana*, or underground apartment, from which, a few days before the disastrous expedition to Chinhutt, an immense quantity of jewels, plate and gold and silver ornaments set with precious stones, were secured, by Major Banks, the Commissioner, and conveyed in safety into the Residency: the whole mass afterwards realized nearly a million sterling at a public auction in Calcutta. In respect to these jewels, the action of Major Banks was most praiseworthy and determined: the Major, armed with orders from Sir Henry Lawrence, who had positive information of the existence of the treasure, requested a certain functionary, named Miftah-ood-dowlah, who was the actual custodian, to allow him to see the treasure: the man positively denied all knowledge of the existence of such a treasure; but on the Major drawing his revolver and threatening to shoot the fellow, he become nervous, and calling for lights, led the way, in a faltering manner, down a flight of steps into the underground room, where the treasure was found packed in a number of antique looking boxes. This apartment also contained a vast quantity of valuable articles, such as silver howdahs, chairs, bedsteads and other rich property which, unfortunately, there was no time to remove. Miftah-ood-dowlah evidently expected assistance from a number of *Seedees*, Africans, the King's retainers, who were present, but the precaution had been taken to form up a battery of Artillery and a body of Infantry in position, whilst the Major entered the *tykhana*, accompanied by thirty picked volunteers. When the mutineers entered Lucknow a few days afterwards, greedy for plunder, much to their chagrin, they found the *tykhana* empty: they, however, seized upon, and occupied, Kaiser Bagh, appropriating the valuable furniture, jewels, dresses and other property of the ex-King and the opulent ladies of the Court, making the most terrible havoc throughout the sumptuously fitted suites of ladies' apartments.

Leaving the Western gate, a large four-storied building, surmounted by a gilt semicircle and, originally, a gilt hemisphere or semi-dome, is seen. This is the—

KAISER PUSSUND.

VIEW NO. 27.

The house of "*Cæsar's pleasure.*" This fantastic building belonged to Roshun-ood-dowlah, King Naseer-ood-deen Hyder's Prime Minister, but Wajid Ali Shah, the last King of Oudh, took possession of it, under what understanding is not known, and placed it at the disposal of a favourite *Mehal*, Maushookos Sultan, for her residence. It was in the *tykhanas*, or underground chambers, of this building, that the British captives, Miss Jackson, Mrs. Green, and the rest, were confined, up to the time they were led out to the front of the gateway, already described, to be publicly and barbarously murdered.

The interior of the Kaiser Pussund was originally decorated sumptuously and furnished with the usual Oriental magnificence; the exterior still has a very palatial appearance, as may be seen from the view; but the whole pile has been for years past, and is still, put to a very different use to what it was intended to serve: its spacious and lofty rooms are now turned into the offices of the Treasury, City Superintendent of Police, the Courts of the Deputy Commissioner, the City Magistrate and others. The structure must have cost an immense sum, and may be taken as a fair specimen of the notorious extravagance of the rulers of Oudh.

To the right, at the end of this road, is a small arch known as—

NEIL'S GATE.

VIEW NO. 28.

This arch was formerly called "*Share Darwaza*, or Tiger's Gate. The history of the extraordinary feats of arms, the unprecedented boldness, the reckless bravery of that gallant soldier, General Neil, has already filled the world with astonishment. With a small force, he traversed the country, and, in all the terrible engagements he fought, never knew defeat. His name struck terror into the hearts of the rebels, the mere mention of "Neil" caused trembling and flight. That resolute soldier, in his unbroken career of conquest, saved station after station, relieved Allahabad, and, to the amazement and consternation of the enemy, pursued them so rapidly, that they had the greatest difficulty to escape. In pursuance of the inexorable determination and energy which characterized him, he advanced to the relief of Lucknow, and while leading his numerically diminutive, but valiant, followers through the gate, shown in the view, to the rescue of the beleaguered Garrison, in which he knew there were not only British soldiers in danger, but ladies and little children; a shot from a battery of the enemy's in Kaiser Bagh struck him, and deprived England of as intrepid and successful a soldier as she ever possessed.

To mark the spot where he fell, there certainly ought to be a monument, or something better than the wretched little arch, seen in the view; however, General Neil was not the man to claim honors from his country; his pride lay in the knowledge of having done his duty; and he did it well.

Beyond this spot, is the ground on which formerly stood the barracks of a Police Battalion, under command of Captain Adolphus Orr. This Battalion rebelled, and in their pursuit poor Thornhill, of the Civil Service, a son-in-law of Sir Henry Havelock, received a wound, which proved mortal.

Further to the North, spanning the river Goomtee, is—

BRUCE'S BRIDGE.

View No. 29.

There was formerly a bridge of boats here; the present bridge was built in 1865, and completed in 1866, under the superintendence of Mr. Bruce, the then Municipal Engineer. The work can hardly be said to have turned out an engineering success, since, during the flood season of 1870, the north side wing pier was cut under by the current and gave way: it has since been repaired and is open for traffic, but its permanency is questionable, since the plan upon which it is built seems adapted to a tidal river, rather than a river subject to floods, like the Goomtee. The old stone bridge, built nearly a hundred years ago, may be placed in contrast, it preserves its original solidity, and it will be described hereafter.

To the west on the banks of the river, appears a pile of buildings called the—

CHUTTER MUNZIL.

View Nos. 30 and 31.

This consists of a number of very handsome, lofty buildings, the chief of which is imposingly situated on the right bank of the Goomtee; it is conspicuous, especially on account of its *chutter*, or umbrella, which, covered with gold, glitters in the sun, at a great height, above the building. This enormous *parachute* gives the name to the whole group of buildings. In architecture, these structures are a pleasing mixture of the Oriental geometrical, the Italian, and the French *chateau*: they were built, at a fabulous expense, by King Nascer-ood-deen Hyder, as residences for his numerous *Mehals* or Queens. At that time they were surrounded by a high masonry wall, and afforded a powerful stronghold for the rebels in 1857-58. The tremendous amount of battering necessary to dislodge the mutineers from this position, before it could be taken, would hardly be believed by any one that was not actually present with Sir Henry Havelock's force.

The largest of the buildings is now the United Service Club, a most elegant *restaurant*, delightfully cool in the summer months and offering the best accommodation, such even the clubs of Pall Mall might envy : it may also be considered the Town Hall of Lucknow, since public meetings, balls, *soirées*, and committees are held there. The other buildings, all four-storied, are used as public offices ; the Small Cause Court, and Civil Court &c.

Close by, on the same road, is the—

LAL BARADURREE.

View No. 32.

The common name of this building, *Kasrool Khakan*, or King's house, conveys no description of what it was used or intended for. Leaving religion out of the question, it may be considered the "Westminster Abbey" of Oudh. It was the Throne Room, the Coronation Hall, and Grand Durbar, or Hall of Assembly, of the monarchs of Oudh. It takes its name from the colour of the stone, with which it is built, or the plastering with which it is covered, being red. From the time of Saadut-Ali Khan, all coronations took place in the great hall of this "*Lal Baradurree.*"

As will be seen from the view, the plan of the architects was to make the building colossal ; in keeping with the purpose for which it was intended, but although a fine structure, it falls far behind the Athenian or Roman Models.

From the history of Oudh, it will be remembered that a dispute to the succession took place between Moonna Jan, the pretender, and Naseer-ood-dowlah ; the people were in a state of intense excitement, the argument in the Lal Baradurree was fast approaching a riot; the usurper attempted to coerce the British Resident into acknowledging his right to the succession; the Resident, Colonel Lowe, resolutely refused to present the accustomed *nuzzur*, or offering, to Moonna Jan, and finding a number of insurgents about the place, gave orders for cannon to be brought to bear on the building, and would undoubtedly have reduced it to ruins, had not Moonna Jan, with his mother, the Badsha Begum, and all their followers, made their escape, leaving Nussur-ood-dowlah in undisputed possession of the throne.

The grandest *Durbar* ever known in Lucknow was held in the Lal Baradurree: it took place on the triumphal entry of Lord Canning into the capital; every noble in Oudh was present in his most glaring costume, resplendent with jewellery, the staff of the Governor-General was extremely brilliant; probably neither before nor since has so picturesque a scene been witnessed in the Lal Baradurree.

The result of that Durbar formed a new era in the history of Oudh; the nobles were clearly given to understand who were their Governors, and what was the policy of the British Government.

The Lal Baradurree is kept, by the British Government, in a state of good preservation, and is used up to the present day for the purpose of holding durbars, whenever such assemblies are necessary.

The same road leads to a spot that will ever be held sacred in history: it is the—

BAILIE GUARD.

VIEWS NOS. 33 AND 34.

From such a poor common name very little can be gathered, but really there is no name that can be given;

no poetry could describe, no pen could narrate, adequately, the terrible bloody, but glorious history of that place, that *Aceldama*, called the Bailie Guard. The histories of battles and sieges, such as Alma, Inkermann and Sebastopol are comparatively ephemeral, evanescent as flashes of lightning in a passing thunder-storm; but the history of the defence made by the Lucknow Garrison, in the Bailie Guard, will live for ever.

To the scene of the ground upon which the Lucknow Garrison sustained a siege of unparalleled severity for seven months, hemmed in by a barbarous and relentless foe, thirsting, like wolves, for blood and, like mercenary fanatics, for treasure, the entrances are now ordinary carriage drives; and, without explanation, the traveller can see but little that will convey an adequate idea of the sufferings and hardships, encountered and overcome at such a terrible sacrifice, by the glorious Garrison, truly described by the "*Bayard of India*" as "more than illustrious."

The term "Bailie Guard" owes its origin to a Resident of the Court of Oudh, Colonel Bailie, whose official escort of troops used to be located at the gate leading to the Residency. During the siege, this gate was blocked up with sandbags, and barricades were erected behind it: it was then called a "post," or point of defence, and was placed in charge of Lieutenant Aitkin of the 13th Native Infantry; a few men of his corps remained loyal and cast in their lot, for good or for evil, along with him; with their help, he defended the position most gallantly throughout, performing acts of incredible bravery: he was rewarded with the Victoria Cross, and is now Colonel and Inspector-General of Police, Oudh, a recognition which he well deserves.

Passing the building formerly used by the ex-King as stables for his Arabian horses, now the Lucknow Museum, the archway (View No. 33) comes in sight; this was fortified, and for five months the shot and shell of the enemy could make no impression on it, and it withstood successfully their most furious attacks. This archway was the proper entrance to the Residency: it was through it that the brave relieving force marched with the gallant Outram at their head, on the 25th of September, 1857. The General was wounded early in the day, but still kept his place in the saddle and remained at the head of his column. On this event, the enthusiasm of the defenders has been graphically described by Sir George Couper; it put new life into them just at a time when they considered their fate sealed and had given up all hope. General Outram was the first man who entered the Bailie Guard to effect the memorable "*relief of Lucknow.*" Every man who could stand upon his feet joined in giving hearty British cheers at the entrance of that force which proclaimed to them that they were saved from a fate worse than death. Women and children then experienced that blessed sense of security which only those who have encountered, and been providentially saved from, imminent peril, can possibly appreciate. Native and European congratulated each other; mothers folded their darling children to their breasts; and an earnest prayer of thanksgiving arose to Heaven. For Outram and Havelock, it seemed at that moment, that a draught of immortality had been drunk from the Divine stream; they are now in their honored graves; the memory of their gallant deeds dwells, in sincere gratitude, in the hearts of the survivors of that Garrison; and, as companions in arms on earth, it is the earnest prayer of all that they may be companions of angels in heaven. Stars of the battle-field, where the sword and bayonet glittered in the charge and death-fires flashed, they calmly smiled at the foe, wrenched from the cowardly rebels the sceptre of monarchy which they had assumed, and dashed them into the slough of despond, which they had themselves prepared for the British.

It is necessary here to notice the disastrous expedition to Chinhutt, because it was from the date of this battle that the siege of the Bailie Guard commenced. The head of the intelligence department was the Finanical Commissioner, Martin Gubbins, who learned that a body of rebels were threatening Lucknow, but it appears had no accurate information of their strength. The British force was most inadequate, consisting only of a small body of infantry, some volunteer cavalry, a few field guns, and an eight-inch howitzer drawn by an elephant; Newab Mohsin-ood-dowlah, grandson of Ghazee-ood-deen Hyder, the first King of Oudh, sent elephants, carts and other conveyances to assist the expedition, which marched off under a tropical sun on a hot morning in the month of June. The rebel forces were encountered at a distance of six miles, but to the surprise of the British, an army of infantry, cavalry and artillery, calculated at sixty thousand strong, regularly organized, drilled and disciplined with a Commander-in-Chief and full staff, was formed up. A check was given for a moment to the enemy's advance, by a spirited charge of the volunteer cavalry; the rebels were taught by this to keep a respectful distance; treating the small British force like hornets that could sting sharp, but that they would much like to catch, they tried hard to surround the diminutive body by out-flanking; and the British, seeing this movement, were compelled to retreat, abandoning their guns, elephants and carriage, and leaving Colonel Case and nearly one hundred men of Her Majesty's 32nd amongst the killed. Lieutenant-Colonel Inglis was in command, but the fatal movement was principally directed by Sir Henry Lawrence. The force retreated at once into the Bailie Guard and the siege commenced. It was from a shell, from the same eight-inch howitzer which thus fell into the possession of the rebels at the battle of Chinhutt, that Sir Henry Lawrence, whilst seated in a room on the north-east corner of the Residency, received his death-wound on the third day after the commencement of the siege. He died on the third or fourth day afterwards. Sensible to the last, his final request was, that nothing should be inscribed on his tomb except the words—

"HERE LIES HENRY LAWRENCE,

Who tried to do his duty;

MAY THE LORD HAVE MERCY ON HIS SOUL."

Leaving the small, grim-looking archway, which formed the principal entrance to the Residency (View No. 33), on the south is the site of the Post Office Garrison, where Major Anderson of the Bengal Engineers died from long sickness, and where the brave Mace of Her Majesty's 32nd also expired from the effects of wounds received while leading a sortie on the Cawnpore road.

Adjoining, was Sago's Garrison where Bryson, a brave volunteer, was shot while endeavouring to repair a gap in the roof; a little above this, was the Judicial Garrison, a very important, but much exposed post, defended by Sikhs and volunteers who fought desperately. On the opposite side of the road, the enemy held a very strong position behind loop-holed walls, where, secure from British bullets, they kept up an incessant galling fire on the Garrison, which was thus placed almost at their mercy. The enemy made many determined attempts to enter the entrenchment at this spot, but were invariably repulsed by its brave defenders under Major Gorman, 13th Native Infantry. Here Lieutenant Green of the same regiment died from exhaustion caused by the severity of his duties; and one brave volunteer was shot through the head.

A few yards to the south was Anderson's out-post which, from its position, close to the Cawnpore Battery, was terribly exposed to the fire of the enemy: the roof was battered down, falling on the heads of the defenders. The Commandant, Captain Anderson, 25th Native Infantry, and Mr. Capper,

C. S., now a Commissioner in Oudh, were literally buried in the ruins, but were dug out, alive and not much hurt.

A little to the rear of the Cawnpore Battery was Dupratt's Garrison. M. Dupratt was a French gentleman of indomitable and even reckless courage. His manner towards the enemy was not only defiant in the extreme, but by gesture and vociferous, or positively insulting, language, he tried his hardest to exasperate the rebels and thus cause them, in the height of their rage, to expose themselves in an attempt at a futile attack, hurriedly organized ; and many a mutineer bit the dust, through the extraordinary system of tactics adopted by this brave and enthusiastic Frenchman. It was M. Dupratt who received overtures from the miscreant Nana Saheb, offering him a "command" of a most important nature in the rebel army. To the everlasting honor of the French nation, be it recorded, that M. Dupratt scornfully rejected the offer. He was at length killed by a shot, whilst gallantly defending his post.

Near to this spot are the ruins of a building that was occupied by the Martiniere boys, who, under command of their Principal, rendered valuable service by attending the sick and wounded, and performing various duties, such as grinding corn, &c., conducing much towards the comfort of the besieged : they were also brave and active in defending their post, firing well directed vollies at the enemy. Many of those boys, now men, may be recognized, in the ranks of the present Lucknow Rifle Volunteer Corps, their breasts displaying the honors they won in the memorable siege of the Bailie Guard.

The Cawnpore Battery, the position of which has already been pointed out, was considered as desperate and dangerous a post to hold as any in the whole line of defences ; here, as elsewhere, the enemy made frantic, though futile, attempts to carry the place by storm. Hand-grenades, thrown amongst the crowds of yelling fanatics, dealt death and destruction, and inflicted such ghastly and excruciating wounds that an ignominious retreat, leaving heaps of dead and wounded, was nearly always the result. The defenders, however, did not escape scatheless. In this battery, Lieutenants Lavin and Alexander of the Artillery, Lieutenant Arthur and Captain Radcliffe, of the 7th Cavalry, were mortally wounded; and many other valuable lives were lost in defending this post. Respecting Captain Radcliffe, it may be here related, that it was on the memorable day of the "RELIEF," while all hearts were rejoicing at the arrival of the gallant succouring force, that that brave and indefatigable officer, after surviving nearly three months' hard work and exposure, at various outposts, received his death-wound; a calamity which converted the transient joy of the defenders into inexpressible sorrow, for he was as much admired and loved by friends, as he was feared by the enemy. It was Radcliffe, who as Commandant of the Volunteer Company, with only about forty men, brought up the rear of the fugitive column from Chinhutt, successfully keeping at bay the relentless rebels, who were in hot pursuit on all sides.

Next is a spot, called during the siege "Sikh's Square," especially remarkable as having been the scene of one of the most extraordinary escapes ever known in the annals of battles and sieges. The enemy here sprung a mine, blowing Captains Alexander, Orr and Mecham, into the air. Those officers fell on the enemy's side of the defences, but, being providentially unhurt, contrived to regain their own entrenchment in safety. Ten Christian drummers, who were lying asleep when the explosion took place, were, however, less fortunate; the poor fellows were buried under the ruins of a fallen building. The astonishing conduct of the enemy on this occasion may be taken as an amusing illustration of the deplorable incapacity of the natives of Hindustan generally for anything like active warfare, except when led by European officers and supported by European troops. The springing of this mine opened a breach broad enough for a column of infantry to have dashed through; and had they followed up the advantage thus gained, the enemy would have secured possession of the post without striking a single blow, and would, or might, have opened the way to the capture of the whole Garrison; but, on the contrary, the rebels appeared astounded at the demolition effected by their own work, and fled from the spot with the utmost precipitation.

Separated from this by a high wall, stand the ruins of the Brigade Mess-house, which was used as the Head Quarters of Brigadier Inglis, Commandant of the Garrison: the post was a commanding one, from which the rifles of some of the officers kept the rebels in effectual check, and prevented them from making any serious attacks on the defences to the right and left. When the breach was opened by the explosion of the mine, described above, it appears that the Sikhs, who occupied part of the square, fled; and except for the hot fire kept up from the Brigade Mess-house, there was nothing to prevent the enemy from passing through the breach, but their own cowardice.

On the right stood what were known as the "ladies' quarters," and immediately fronting those buildings, are the ruins of Mr. Ommaney's house; this was considered tolerably safe, notwithstanding the fact that, Mr. Ommaney was killed in it, during the early part of the seige, by a stray shot from one of the enemy's batteries, close to the entrenchment on the westward.

Almost adjoining this on the left, is Mr. Gubbins, the Financial Commissioner's, house. This was really a small fortress in itself, the redoubtable Gubbins acting as his own commandant, although Major Ashton, 41st Native Infantry, claimed and enjoyed the honor of the post. The building was in a very exposed position, affording the enemy prominent marks for the exercise of their artillery and musketry. It was against this house, that the rebels exploded a mine on the occasion of the last and most desperate general assault made on the entire entrenchment. It was here that the gallant Lieutenant Fulton, of the Engineers, after braving the dangers and privations of the siege, almost to the end, after working mine and countermine, to the surprise and consternation of the enemy, for months, was shot through the head, whilst reconnoitering the enemy's positions. It was here too that Major Banks the Commissioner, whom Sir Henry Lawrence on his death-bed, had nominated as his successor, was shot through the head, before he had been many days in the position assigned him; a position for which opinion was unanimous that he was admirably fitted. Here also, Mr. Cameron, a Calcutta merchant, sank under exhaustion caused by excessive hard work at the batteries. Dr. Brison also, who had escaped all the horrors of the Cabul massacre and the dangers of the Khyber Pass, was mortally wounded by a shot through the back received while sitting at dinner at Mr. Gubbins' table. Mrs. Dorin, widow of Captain Dorin, of the 41st, who was murdered by the mutineers at Seetapore; had made her escape to Lucknow disguised as an *ayah*, was killed by a round shot, whilst in bed in Mr. Gubbins' house. Poor Mr. Gubbins himself survived the horrors of the siege only to meet a more melancholy fate; the unfortunate gentleman put an end to his own life whilst in a state of temporary insanity: such was the stern decree of fate, to which all must yield. Martin Gubbins has, however, left behind him a deathless memorial in the best written and most authoritative work on the "Mutinies of Oudh," in which the siege of Lucknow is graphically described. The book, will, as ages pass in succession, like the epic history of the siege of Troy, which long lay neglected, be read with increasing interest and excitement.

Turning to the right, from Gubbins' house; in full view stand the ruins of the "Old Residency," in all the melancholy grandeur of a once magnificent mansion, in all the

6

superb beauty of mournful decay. The structure was erected by Saadut Ali Khan, King of Oudh, for the express purpose of a palatial dwelling for the British Resident at the Court of Oudh, and the king seems to have spared no pains to produce an edifice that, with its subordinate buildings, should possess all architectural characteristics of royalty, and a view of the ruins will not fail to convince the beholder that His Majesty succeeded. During the siege, the spacious *tykhana* was occupied by the families of Her Majesty's 32nd regiment. In consequence of the open space around the Residency, the people of the garrison could not leave, or go to the building, without risking their lives, for the clear ground was constantly swept by shot, shell and bullets, and the enemy kept a sharp lookout for any one attempting to pass; the building itself also formed a convenient target for the rebels to point their guns at, as the result clearly testified. The severe cannonading, to which the Residency was subjected, brought down the roof of the eastern verandah, burying seven men of Her Majesty's 32nd, in the ruins; two of these were extricated alive, the remainder perished. Ensign Studdie of Her Majesty's 32nd, amongst numerous others, was killed here; poor Miss Palmer, being one of the number.

To the east are to be seen the dismantled and shattered walls of what was once the "Banqueting Hall;" the massive columns which supported the roof still standing and forming, at a single view, a truly majestic ruin; many a brave warrior, many a proud statesman and many a patrician beauty have met in courtly assembly here, have joined in the mazy dance, and made the walls ring with merry laughter, little imagining what was so soon to be the sad fate of the noble structure. During the siege, it was converted into a hospital, but, as a two-storied building, it was, on account of its height, much exposed to the enemy's fire: in the words of Sir George Couper:—"Round shot and shell crashed into it from all sides" and the upper story was, in a few days, rendered utterly untenable; the basement rooms were consequently crammed to suffocation; there the enervated sick and wounded of the feeble garrison languished and died amid all the miseries engendered by wounds, foul atmosphere, disease, confinement and, worse than all, suspense and its companion despair. Further, the lower story was not secure from the enemy's round shot and musketry: many of the sufferers were shot in their beds. None but those who witnessed that scene, can form an adequate idea of the anguish, misery and horror that existed. Let it be said here, that those who were able, in any way, to afford assistance in mitigating the sufferings of the doomed unfortunates, did so most readily and cheerfully; and may it be remembered to their honour. The Reverend Mr. Polehampton ministered to the spiritual wants of the sick and wounded with creditable assiduity, until at length he was carried off himself; but in what manner, history is conflicting; one account says that he received a bullet in the breast while sitting beside a wounded man, another account states that he died from cholera: his widow, however, survived the siege.

A short distance in advance, between the Residency and the Banqueting Hall, on the summit of a grassy mound, stands the "LAWRENCE MEMORIAL," a simple but handsome pillar of chunar stone, designed by, and executed under the superintendence of Mr. Cuthbert Thornhill, Commissioner of Allahabad. It was inaugurated in 1864, and the address, delivered on the occasion by Sir George Couper, was thrilling in the extreme; penetrating to the hearts of the survivors, who knew Sir Henry and had fought with him, and of whom many were present. The spot upon which the monument is erected is not remarkable for any incidents connected with the siege: it was an open space, very dangerous to cross, and it was in attempting to cross this plain, that poor Captain Graidon was literally riddled with bullets, causing instantaneous death.

The memorial bears the following inscription :—

TO THE MEMORY OF

MAJOR GENERAL SIR HENRY LAWRENCE, K. C. B.

AND THE

BRAVE MEN WHO FELL

IN DEFENCE OF THE RESIDENCY,

A. D., 1857.

On the right is the site of the Redan Battery, which was as redoubtable as its great namesake at Sebastopol, in its own way. The Redan on the north, the Cawnpore Battery on the south, and the Mortar Battery at the Post Office, acting in conjunction, were the salvation of the apparently doomed garrison. The Redan commanded the passage over the Iron Bridge, which will be noticed presently, and kept in check the enemy's batteries at Dil-auram and Badshah Bagh which, with those on the west, posted in mosques on the summits of mounds, played with deadly effect on the Residency: the Redan was commanded by Lieutenant Lawrence of Her Majesty's 32nd throughout the whole siege. That fearless officer was wounded several times, but, happily, recovered from his injuries.

The sites of the most important outposts and positions have now been treated of, but, at present, those posts are merely indicated by sign-posts, nothing remaining to mark their situation. After a lapse of seventeen years it will be easily understood, that a cursory examination of the ground, which has undergone so many changes, will not afford any conception of what the Bailie Guard was at the time of the siege. At the commencement, the whole of the defences or entrenchments, if they might be called such, consisted of a shallow ditch a few feet in breadth, the actual entrenchments were formed in great haste and by immense labour ; as the siege progressed, the garrison were made aware of their weak points and strengthened them, to the best of their power, so that the defences became, day after day, more and more formidable. On the re-occupation of Lucknow, the several earthworks forming outposts, batteries, &c., were levelled, an embankment was raised and a ditch dug, encircling the whole entrenchment, giving it the appearance of a fortified camp-ground, but entirely destroying the original appearance of the lines of defences, and, so far, consigning to oblivion the important reminiscences and interesting associations which, at least in the memory of the present generation, will remain attached, and deeply engraven on the hearts of the survivors. Sir Colin Campbell declared the Bailie Guard to be a "*false position,*" and his opinion should have been sufficient to deter the authorities from giving the spot the appearance of a preparation for future defence. When this error was pointed out to Lord Canning, both in a political and military point of view, he permitted the ruins to remain as they stood, and the whole of the enclosure to be laid out in ornamental, floral walks. The Bailie Guard is now consecrated ground. The bodies of the brave men and women who fell during the siege and were buried there, were, after the final relief, torn from their graves by the mutineers and scattered about, the whole place was dug up in the mad search for treasure, so that on the re-occupation not a trace of the graves, and indeed hardly a vestige of the original order of things remained. However the place is now very prettily laid out, there is a well kept cemetery and, without these pleasant additions to such a mournful spot, the ruins themselves are more than sufficient to repay the visit of the most indifferent tourist.

Adjoining on the south is the recently erected

BULRAMPORE HOSPITAL.

VIEW No. 35.

The spot upon which this hospital now stands is, in history, closely connected with the Bailie Guard; Phillips' house was on this very ground; it was one of the strongest positions, in the enemy's occupation, on the Cawnpore road side. After the arrival of the relieving force, this formidable stronghold was stormed and taken, by a hundred volunteers, from different Corps, under command of Lieutenant Colonel Haliburton of Her Majesty's 78th Highlanders who, after occupying the place for two days, was killed, and the enemy pressed, in such irresistible force,that the position had to be abandoned and many lives were lost before that obstinate little force got back into the old entrenchments.

The munificence of the Maharajah of Bulrampore is notorious: the spot upon which so many lives were recklessly lost, is now devoted by that philanthrophic nobleman, to the saving of lives. The hospital has been built not as an object of architectural beauty to perpetuate the name of the donor, but on the latest improved plan, having sole regard to the comfort of the inmates; it is not a single block, on the old principle, but a number of detached buildings admitting free ventilation and fresh air from any direction. A Medical Training College has, since the opening of the hospital, been established, thus rendering the institution thoroughly complete. This valuable addition is also endowed by Sir Drig Bijoy Singh, K. G. C. S. I., Maharajah of Bulrampore, whose noble and disinterested charities, must reflect the highest credit on his name, and render his memory imperishable.

From the Bulrampore Hospital may be seen the—

IRON BRIDGE.

VIEW No. 36.

This handsome bridge was sent out from England, by sections complete, in the year 1816, but the death of the importer put a stop to the undertaking: Saadut Ali Khan died about two years before its arrival, and the work long remained suspended, because the king was reluctant to complete a project commenced by his predecessor. After tho lapse of about thirty years, when Mohummed Ali Shah came to the throne, the bridge was erected and now forms a conspicuous ornament to the city. The British force crossed this bridge, in the retreat from Chinhutt and, as it could be swept by the cannon from the Residency, the persuing rebels were terribly cut up in following. However, crossing the bridge did not finish the Chinhutt disaster, for, in passing the narrow streets on their way to the entrenchment, about fifty men were cut off by the rebels who fired from the housetops and could not be got at. Had the enemy known of the Chinhutt defeat, they might have taken possession of the Iron Bridge, and so have cut off the retreat of the British, in which case, the Garrison, containing some four or five hundred men, women and children would have fallen into their hands. The bridge several times suffered a severe battering, but appears now not at all disfigured, and it serves as a convenient means of transit.

At the north-western extremity of the city appears the—

STONE BRIDGE.

VIEW No. 37.

This Bridge was built by Newab Ausuf-ood-dowlah, about the year 1780. It is a substantial structure and has proved its durability by not requiring any repairs since it was built. It has no particular claims to architectural beauty, but the view from its parapets, up and down the river Goomptee, is extremely picturesque. Many inaccuracies concerning this river have crept into history. Heber described it as a broad and rapid river. Wordsworth, on the contrary, said it was a narrow insignificant stream, the water of which was undrinkable on account of the quantity of yellow earth, or mud, held in solution: he further observed that, when sickness prevailed in the city, the water became poisonous and a quantity of putrid scum floated on the surface from the number of dead bodies thrown into it. The truth is, that the Goomptee takes its rise in the swamps of Pillibheet on the borders of Oudh; in the flood season it is broad and rapid; in the dry season it sometimes almost disappears.

It is navigable, almost to its source and falls into the Ganges near Patna. The water is pure and, when filtered, drinkable as that of other rivers in India.*

LUCHMAN TELA

OR

MUCHEE BHAWUN.

VIEW No. 38.

This Fort is adjacent to the stone bridge; it stands on an eminence and is supposed to be the original centre around which the city of Lucknow sprang up. Two centuries have elapsed since it was made into a fort, and it may now be considered as the citadel of Lucknow. After the annexation, many alterations and improvements were made, and it was strongly garrisoned, but it never gave much promise of strength. There is an old tradition to the effect that, he who holds Muchee Bhawun might, in time of trouble, safely

* Between Ghazepur and Banaras.

reckon upon an army, as numerous as the fish in the Goomtee, to rally round his standard: a tradition that proved significantly false, in the case of the British, for, instead of the traditional army making its appearance, the troops deserted by whole regiments at a time and not a single man could be induced to join the ranks of the British force, after the rebellion had once commenced.

In 1857, Muchee Bhawun was well stored with gunpowder, ammunition and ordnance supplies of all descriptions, and from these, precautions had been taken to well stock the Residency. After the battle of Chinhutt, it soon became apparent that the fort was untenable; it was therefore resolved to evacuate it and blow it up. This movement was successfully accomplished on the night of the 1st July, 1857. The small body of troops located there were quietly formed up, a time fuze, cut for twenty minutes-was fixed in the magazine and lighted. The party then marched off; the fuze had been timed, so as to allow them to reach the Bailie Guard before the explosion should take place; it was well timed, for exactly at the twentieth minute it did take place; a tremendous explosion which caused the earth to rock as from a mighty earthquake, which shook every house to its foundations and which struck terror and consternation into the hearts of the rebels. The party from Muchee Bhawun reached the Bailie Guard and joined their comrades, in safety. The falling debris must have caused much damage and loss of life in the city, but not a soul in the Bailie Guard was hurt. After the re-occupation of Lucknow, Muchee Bhawun was rebuilt; it is now a fort of considerable strength, armed with heavy guns, and garrisoned by both artillery and infantry.

The gate to the west was, prior to the siege, a place of public execution for mutineers; on this spot, many a rebel paid the last penalty of the law as a punishment for his perfidy to the British Government.

The small mosque, on the opposite side of the ruin, is of some importance, since it marks the mound originally called Luchman Tela: a name conferred upon it, long before Lucknow became the capital of Oudh.

In the immediate vicinity of the Muchee Bhawan is the—

GREAT IMAMBARA
OF
NAWAB AUSUF-OOD-DOWLAH.

VIEWS NOS. 39 TO 41.

Nawab Ausuf-ood-dowlah was the first monarch of Oudh and he it was, who made Lucknow the capital. The great Imambara was built by him; and it is justly pronounced to be the architectural gem of the city, its minarets are the tallest and handsomest, and it is the most magnificent and massive structure in Lucknow. The central hall is supposed to be the largest in the world, but the most remarkable feature of the building is, that it contains no wood-work of any kind, being built throughout, exclusively of solid masonry. It is said to have cost a crore of rupees, or one million sterling, a doubtful tradition, unless it was originally embellished with precious stones, of which however there is now no trace. According to Elliott, the story is, that Nawab Ausuf-ood-dowlah invited architects, throughout India, to submit plans, to be subjected to competition, for an Imambara, stipulating that the building should not be a copy of any other building, and that, in beauty and magnificence, it should surpass anything of the kind that ever was in existence. The name given to the successful competition is Kifait-ool-lah and, on viewing the structure, it must be admitted that his conception has produced a thing of beauty and a stupendous solidity, or massive grandeur, in happy keeping with the purpose for which it was intended, that is, a mausoleum for the interment of the King himself. The building will hardly bear comparison with the Taj at Agra, the designs being of quite a diverse order, the one is remarkable for the beauty of its configuration and intricacy of its embellishments, the other for the solemnity of its contour and colossal grandeur of its preparations; both are, however, as superb curiosities, equally worthy of a visit.

It has been the custom of Mohumedan potentates to provide, before their death, for the maintenance of the Imambaras, that were to contain their remains, by a rich endowment, but in this case, Nawab Ausuf-ood-dowlah seems to have neglected this important matter, hence the splendid building is now used as a gun-shed and ordnance store, a purpose that its illustrious founder certainly never anticipated it would be put to. It now stands as a monument of the utter futility of monarchs attempting to perpetuate their names and continue, after their demise. a sort of travestie of the courtly extravagance that caused them to be flattered and worshipped in life.

Leaving the Great Imambara, on the way to the next Imambara, an archway has to be passed. This is called the—

ROOMEE DURWAZA.

VIEW NO. 42.

This is supposed to be a model, or copied reconstruction, of an archway now standing in one of the principal streets of Constantinople, as to whether it is such, is doubtful: it was built by Nawab Ausuf-ood-dowlah, and it is possible that monarch may have been the victim of a deception; however, it was represented to him as such, and anything coming, or professing to come, from the capital of the Sultan, the head of the faith, must needs be a valuable acquisition. Hence it was erected, and whether it is or is not what is set forth, it is an ornament to one of the broadest and most fashionable streets in Lucknow. It has no especial historical associations connected with it.

To the right is the Dowlat Khana, the Palace of Nawab Ausuf-ood-dowlah; it comprises many buildings which after the annexation were used by the British as ordnance and commissariat stores; on the breaking out of the rebellion of 1857 they were abandoned.

Proceeding to the end of the grand street, a little beyond is seen the entrance to the—

HOOSAIN-ABAD IMAMBARA.

VIEWS NOS. 43 TO 46.

The entrance is on the left; a huge archway guarded by two of the most frightful looking sphynxes imaginable; within the enclosure is, "THE IMAMBARA," where lie the remains of Mohumed Ali Shah, King of Oudh, and grandfather of the present ex-King, Wajid Ali Shah; the remains of Mohumed Ali Shah's mother lie by his side, the tombs of both are overshadowed by a canopy of velvet, fringed with gold and precious stones, the whole interior of the Imambara is crammed with gigantic chandeliers; candelabra, in crystal, springs from the floor, to the height of twelve feet, branching out in all directions, pier-glasses ten feet high stand against the polished marble walls, the pavement, of porphyry and precious stones, is so highly polished that it is almost dangerous to tread upon it, floor, walls, pillars, all are glittering like glass and reflecting floods of light, so that the mind is bewildered in contemplating such an extraordinary scene, surpassing, by far, the stories of the Arabian Nights, and leaving deep in the shade, any accounts of Oriental luxury or grandeur that have ever been recounted, or even exaggerated, by the most enthusiastic travellers. On the anniversary of the King's demise, every year, the Imambara, interior and exterior, the mausoleums of the two Queens, to the right and left, the ornamental garden, tanks, miniature bridges, walls, the principal archway, the buildings outside for the whole distance, to the right and left between the two great archways, the archways themselves with their lofty and gigantic superstructures, the whole of the buildings outside those archways, and the roads leading to them for half a mile each way are all profusely illuminated : millions of lamps are brought into requisition and placed in all possible and in apparently impossible places, towers, kiosks, minarets are all in a blaze, every nook and corner is resplendent ; in the garden, the reflections of myriads of lights are sparkling and scintillating in the water, and the *tout-ensemble*, as viewed from the terraces opposite the Imambara, is so dazzling and fairy-like, that the visitor lost in admiration, imagines himself in the midst of a scene produced by some genius of a supernatural world. At a given signal, a display of fire-works commences, and lasts for more than an hour, an immense number of fire-balloons are sent up, and then the gates are thrown open for the crowds of visitors to enter the Imambara, which, as already described, presents to view, the *ne plus ultra* of splendour, it is literally one mass of gold, silver, crystal and fire. These entertainments are continued for several nights at a cost of about twelve thousand rupees a night, and no doubt the reader will ask, Where does all this money come from ? The question is easily answered. This Imambara, when built by King Mohumed Ali, was endowed with twelve lacs of rupees; during his lifetime he added several large sums to the fund and furnished the building with gold and silver plate, jewels, precious stones and sumptuous furniture, to a fabulous amount; at length, after appointing trustees and an agent, he died and, as he had intended, his remains were interred in this Imambara. The funds afterwards increased until the whole amount, vested in Government four per cent. securities, amounted to thirty-eight lacs, fifty thousand and five hundred rupees, or £38,50,500. It will be seen therefore that Hossain-abad, is very richly endowed, and besides, there are other sources of income, rent of buildings, offerings by rich pilgrims, which amount to a large sum, for Hossain-abad is one of the most brilliant creations ever conceived by the Kings of Oudh, and the Imambara is held especially sacred by all true Mohumedans.

A few words, respecting the fate of the Imambara during the rebellion of 1857-58, will be found by no means uninteresting here. Prior to his death, King Mohumed Ali executed a deed appointing Nawabs Rafeek-ood-dowlah and Azeem-oollah Khan as trustees, and the notorious rebel Shurf-ood-dowlah as agent of the Hossainabad endowment; those three persons seemed to have managed the trust very well, at least for a time, but on the re-occupation of Lucknow, after the rebellion had been stamped out, a number of persons who were entitled to stipends from the endowment, complained to Government that they could not get their money; this led to an enquiry, the result of which was, that it was found that the two trustees and the agent had disappeared; the Imambara had been plundered of all its valuable contents, and the whole of the Government securities, to the amount of thirty-eight and three quarter lacs of rupees had been stolen from the iron safe in which they had been kept in a room attached to the Imambara. Further enquiries discovered Shurf-ood-dowlah, the agent, mortally wounded, his deposition was taken on his death-bed. Eventually one of the trustees, Nawab Rafeek-ood-dowlah, surrendered himself, he was an imbecile old man, stone-blind, the other trustee, Azim-oollah Khan was dead, but his son Ali Buksh Khan represented him. A special court was improvised and the trustees were tried, the trial lasting over a year. The facts elicited were, that on the breaking out of the rebellion, Shurf-ood-dowlah the agent, joined the rebel cause and took rank as Grand Vazeer or Prime Minister in the Rebel Durbar; in this position he dispossessed the trustees and assumed sole control over the whole trust. The rebel government running short of funds, the whole of the gold and silver plate was taken from the Imambara, by order of Prince Birjeesh Kudr, the son of the rebel, Begum Huzrut Mahal, was sent to the mint and coined into money to pay the rebel troops. The trustees, according to their account, were coerced into giving up their seals, under the threat of murdering the son of the elder trustee, the Government securities were taken, and the sinews of war enhanced, by selling some of them to bankers at the rate of 20 per cent. of their actual value. The remainder of the securities fell into the possession of tho rebel Begum and are probably in her possession still. The old trustees were deposed and in their place, the present trustees Nawab Mohsun-ood-dowlah Bahadoor, K. C. S. I., and Nawab Moomtaz-ood-dowlah Bahadoor, were appointed, and in place of Shurf-ood-dowlah, Moonshee Ramprashad was appointed as agent. Government granted duplicates of the missing securities, and now the trust seems to be managed on a very grand and extravagant scale, none the worse for its misfortunes.

Returning from Hossain-abad, on the right is the "*chowk*," or great Bazar: it extends from north to south for about a mile and is entered, at both ends, by an arched gateway. The north gate is called the "Gol Durwaza," the south is known as the "Akbari Durwaza." The latter is said to have been in existence when the Emperor Akbar, of Delhi passed through Lucknow, and on his return, after subduing Nepal, he ordered the arch to be repaired and gave it his name. The chowk is a busy street, but so narrow that a carriage cannot turn in it, hence, none are allowed to enter, but elephants may be seen passing at all hours of the day.

Leaving the chowk and proceeding towards the Chutter Munzil, on the opposite side of the river, is seen the—

DILARAM KOTHEE.

VIEW NO. 47.

This building was erected by Nawab Saadut Ali Khan, there were a number of buildings in connection, but all have been demolished, leaving the present house standing alone. As will be seen from the view, it is a rather handsome building, in the Italian style, three stories high. The King used to retire to this house, after concluding his duties in the Lal Baradurree, so that he might rest there without being disturbed. At that time there were three water-temples standing one on each side, and one in the centre of the river. The King used to sit in the centre one, in the cool of the evening and fish with rod and line; the whole three have been described as elegantly ornamental structures. Those on the banks have disappeared entirely, and all that remains of the centre one, is the masonry pier upon which it stood.

The Dilaram Kothee, standing as it does, with the river in front and the magnificent Chutter Munzil and the group of elegant buildings on the opposite shore, while the back-ground is filled with groves of trees, a more picturesque and even romantic situation could hardly be conceived.

It may be as well to mention here that, in 1857, the rebels had erected a battery, armed with heavy guns, immediately in rear of the house, and those guns dealt terrible destruction in the besieged Bailie Guard; until Sir Colin Campbell arrived. The battery was then stormed, the guns captured by Sir Colin's Higlanders, and the brave crew of H. M.'s S. S. Shannon, who gave no quarter to the mutineers found in possession. The house is now occupied by private persons.

Returning from the Chutter Munzil towards the city, along the Cawnpore road, on the right hand side is found a very handsome mosque, called—

DURGAH HUZRUT ABBAS.

VIEW NO. 48.

This mosque was built by Nawab Saadut Ali Khan, whether for any especial purpose, history does not show. However it is now held sacred by the Shea sect of Mohumedans who resort there, in considerable numbers, to worship. Tradition states the reason of this to have been, that the Nawab Saadut Ali Khan, when visiting the mosque, on one occasion either fell into a trance, or received a sudden awakening. He was, previous to this circumstance, execrated as a tyrant, but he afterwards became a kind, gracious and benign monarch, reigning successfully to the end of his days.

The building being kept in good repair, preserves its original beauty, and is an object that would well repay a visit.

Near to this is another Mohumedan shrine known as—

KAZMAIN.

VIEW NO. 49.

This was built by Shurf-ood-dowlah one of the Deputy Vazeers, in commemoration of his conversion from Hinduism to Mohumedanism. The shrine is interesting, if the story is true, which declares it to be an exact copy of the tomb of the two Imams, Moosa Kazim and Razza Kazim.

These places are well worth a visit when they are illuminated at the celebration of the Mohurrum festival. The sight is then very grand, in fact, defying description.

At some distance along the same road is the—

KURBULLA TAL KATORA.

VIEW No. 50.

This is the place the Mohumedans, of the Shea sect, bury their *tazzias*, at the Mohurrum festival. The *tazzias* are models of the tombs of Mohumed's grandsons at Mecca, the saints, warriors and heroes; they are lightly constructed of bamboo, paper tinsel, talc, &c. The Mohumedans are celebrated for hero-worship, and on this festival everything is done, whether fighting, fasting, feasting or thumping their breasts, in honour of the two brothers Hussan and Hussain, sacred in Mohumedan history, hence the place where the tazzias are buried is sacred also. On the occasion of these interments, thousands of people make it a holiday, forming pic-nic parties along the roads where the tazzias have to pass and the crowds of sight-seers are immense. To the general tourist, in all probability, these thousands of tinsel processions, continuing from morning till night, would be something more than mere curiosities; on festival days then, the Kurbulla Tal Katora is worth visiting; there may not be anything particular to attract visitors at any other time. The history of these festivals and of the persons whose names are repeated, would be too lengthy to insert in this volume. The Guide is therefore respectfully brought to a close with the remark, that although every place of note may not have been inserted, I think if the traveller visits all that are described, both pictorially, and literally, he will be well satisfied with what he has seen and what he possesses, in writing and delineation, regarding the City of Lucknow and its architectural beauties and wonders.

FINIS.

1—Alum Bagh.

2—General Havelock's tomb.

3—Bebeapore ki Kothe.

4—The Wilaite Bagh.

5—Dilkoosha.

6—La. Martiniere.

7—Hyat Buksh,

8—Darus-shafa.

9—Offices of the Oudh & Rohelcund Ry. Co.

10—St. Joseph's Church.

11—Christ's Church.

12—Wingfield park.

13—Sekunder Bagh.

14—Kuddum Russool.

15—Najuf Ashraf or Shah Najaf.

16—Mottee Mahal.

17—Khoorshaid Munzil.

18—Tara Khothe or Star house.

19—Memorial of Massacre of European Captives.

20—Kunkurwali Kothe.

21—Noorbaksh ki Kothe or Light giving house.

22—Gate of Kaiser Bagh.

23—Lunka in the Kaiser Bagh.

24—Bara-duree of Kaiser Bagh.

25—Saadut Ali Khan's Tomb.

26—Moorshud Zadi's Tomb.

27—Kaiser Pussund.

28—Niel's Gate.

29—Bruce's Bridge.

30—Chutter Munzil on brink of the Goomtee.

31—Chutter Munzil the second.

32—Lal Baradurree.

33—Bailie Guard.

34—The inside of Bailie Guard.

35—Bulrampore Hospital.

36—Iron Bridge.

37—Stone Bridge.

38—Luchmau Tela or Muchee Bhawun.

39—Gate of the Great Imambara of Nawab Assuf- ood-daulah.

40—The Principal biulding of the great Imambara. of Nawab Assuf-ood-daulah.

41—Mosque of the great Imambara of Nawab-Assuf-ood-daulah.

42—Roomee Durwaza.

43—First gate of the Hosenabad Imambara.

44—The stone biulding to the Principal biulding of the Hosenabad Imambara,

45—The opposite biulding of the Hosenabad Imam-bara.

46—The Principal biulding of the Hosenabad Imam-bara.

47--Dilaram.

48—Durgah Huzrat Abbass.

49—Kazmain.

50—Kurballa Talkatora,